The Edna Webster Collection
of Undiscovered Writings

Books by Richard Brautigan

Fiction

Trout Fishing in America
A Confederate General from Big Sur
In Watermelon Sugar
The Abortion: An Historical Romance 1966
The Hawkline Monster: A Gothic Western
Willard and His Bowling Trophies: A Perverse Mystery
Sombrero Fallout: A Japanese Novel
Dreaming of Babylon: A Private Eye Novel 1942
The Tokyo–Montana Express
So the Wind Won't Blow It All Away
Revenge of the Lawn

Poetry

The Galilee Hitch-Hiker
Lay the Marble Tea
The Octopus Frontier
All Watched Over by Machines of Loving Grace
Please Plant This Book
The Pill *versus* the Springhill Mine Disaster
Rommel Drives on Deep into Egypt
Loading Mercury with a Pitchfork
June 30th, June 30th

On this the third day of November, 1955, I, Richard Brautigan, give all of my writings to Edna Webster. They are now her property, and she may do what she wishes with them. If she has them published, all of the money derived from publication is hers.

Richard Brautigan

The Edna Webster Collection of Undiscovered Writings

Richard Brautigan

Introduction by Keith Abbott

A MARINER ORIGINAL
Houghton Mifflin Company
Boston • New York
1999

For information about permission to reproduce selec-
tions from this book, write to Permissions, Houghton
Mifflin Company, 215 Park Avenue South, New York,
New York 10003

Library of Congress Cataloging-in-Publication Data

Brautigan, Richard.
  [Selections. 1999]
  The Edna Webster collection of undiscovered
writings / Richard Brautigan ; introduction by
Keith Abbott.
    p.   cm.
Includes index.
ISBN 0-395-97469-0
    I. Webster, Edna. II. Title.   III. Title: Collection
of undiscovered writings
PS3503.R2736 A6 1999
813'.54—dc21   99-32044   CIP

Printed in the United States of America

QUM 10 9 8 7 6 5 4 3 2 1

A hardbound limited edition of this book has been
published by Burton I. Weiss and James Musser.

Contents

Note

I deal in manuscripts and rare books. In October 1992, I got a startling telephone call from a friend who for years had been collecting only one author, Richard Brautigan. He had just received a telephone call from an elderly woman in Oregon who claimed to have been Brautigan's closest friend during his earliest writing days in Eugene. Moreover, her daughter had been his first love, her son his best buddy.

The woman's name was Edna Webster, and she mentioned some things she hoped to sell — unpublished manuscripts mostly, some photographs — all of which Brautigan had given her before starting out at the age of twenty-one for San Francisco. He had assigned the copyrights to her at the same time, and she had a document in Brautigan's hand to prove it. When he gave her the manuscripts, Brautigan said, "When I am rich and famous, Edna, this will be your social security."

My friend the Brautigan collector suspected that if in fact Edna Webster had all that she said she had, the manuscripts alone would be worth much more than he was prepared to spend. So he called me — and in less than an hour, I was on the phone to Eugene. The next day I was on the first plane from San Francisco, arriving at Edna's modest house by noon. We drove to her bank immediately, and opened her safe-deposit box. The contents were fabulous, more than I'd hoped: unpublished photos of Brautigan in the 1950s, his high school diploma, letters from him to Edna and her daughter, and best of all, unpublished manuscripts, including pieces that rank among his best work. By 2:10 we had signed an agreement for the sale of both manuscripts and copyrights. I phoned my bank manager and then took Edna to lunch. (She and I have since become friends.)

A few weeks later, the Bancroft Library at Berkeley bought the Edna Webster Archive. There it joined the manuscripts of

Brautigan's last years, which the library had acquired in 1987.

What follows in this volume has been edited to the extent that duplicate pieces and some of the weaker pieces have been culled. What remains, with only some standardizing of spelling and punctuation, is — unmistakably — just as Brautigan wrote it.

BURTON WEISS

Introduction: Young, Desperate, and in Love

Richard Brautigan's continuing popularity is easy to understand. Brautigan has remained an author the young discover over and over again, much like Saroyan, Salinger, cummings, and Hesse. Between 1967 and 1977, Brautigan's poetry and fiction went through printing after printing, with *Trout Fishing in America* alone selling more than three million copies. During the 1990s, nine of his thirteen books were returned to print and could be seen on campuses everywhere. Brautigan's clear and precise use of language combines with his outrageous humor, outsider stance, and easy irony to connect with generation after generation of readers.

The Edna Webster Collection of Undiscovered Writings contains the work that preceded Brautigan's rocket ride to fame in the late 1960s. These poems and stories give clear indication of how his mind had already fastened on a number of themes and how his comic style was already formed in its characteristic modes: epigrammatic portraits, extended romantic metaphors, precise pictures of daily life. His most pressing theme was love, or the lack of it.

Often his poems were designed to get him a girlfriend. This strategy remained a constant; Brautigan wrote many of his poems because, as an ex-girlfriend once remarked, "Richard was always on the make." (Kenneth Rexroth once opined that poetry functions nobly to ease our passages in and out of love, and that anyone who writes poems for other reasons is out to lunch.)

Brautigan fans will find his other themes here too, mainly in nascent form: acute self-consciousness and the primacy of the individual, the coexistence of cruelty and kindness, the sometimes baffling surrealism of everyday life. Most of all, he writes about the ability of the imagination to transform lives.

This last theme is crucial to understanding Brautigan's work. As the novelist Thomas McGuane once commented, Richard grew up a goofy kid "whose only toy was his brain." Consider "all the cities at once":

> Pretend
> is
> a city
> bigger
> than New York,
> bigger
> than
> all the cities
> at once.

Imagination functioned ambiguously as a savior and a curse. It was at once Brautigan's only hope of survival and the reason for his exile from everyday people, especially during his adolescent years.

Probably the best single description of his adolescence that Brautigan ever wrote can be found in his bleak story, "A Short History of Oregon," in *Revenge of the Lawn*. There he describes his boyhood by means of a lonely, haunted outsider, hitchhiking with a .30-30 rifle in hand during a solo hunting trip. In a patch of logged-off country he comes across a desolate "house-shack," its crude makeshift porch populated by shoeless children who step out to stare at him, wordless in the steady rain, as if a stranger were a thing of wonder.

"I didn't say a word in my passing," Brautigan writes. "The kids were soaking wet now. They huddled together in silence on the porch. I had no reason to believe that there was anything more to life than this."

In his later work he habitually portrayed himself as the loner stuck in low-rent situations; the tall awkward kid who pursued solitary pleasures, such as hunting and fishing; the geek who did not have friends. But here a different picture emerges, that of a young artist trying out various styles borrowed from famous writers — a confident and precocious youth in love, in frustration over the lack of love, and in deep desperation over his status — or non-status — in the world. And underneath it all, the same conclusion: *Kid, get out of town, and fast.*

Richard and I became friends partly because of our common background: a Northwest working-class life. The infrequent personal recollections he shared with me were loaded with heavy doses of rue. To survive and grow as artists, we agreed that flight was our only chance.

Over the nineteen years I knew Brautigan, I never heard him refer to any Northwest people by name — not his sister, mother, father or stepfathers, not his girlfriends or teachers. He never said he graduated from a high school or lived in Eugene. He didn't identify the names of neighborhoods, parks, lakes, or streams, or the names of his church, his schools, or libraries. When he spoke of Oregon, he used generic tags: *a friend, a buddy, two guys I knew, a spinster who lived nearby.* All these were left without identification, existing as phantoms of a previous life.

The effect was ghostly, as if Brautigan's past had faded into a kind of surrealist museum whose holdings were indicated only by chalk outlines. These outlines gave off the strong suggestion of crime, of accidents and injury. They hinted at painful events and terrors and tortured relationships, but only rarely did Brautigan confirm them, and then often in an abstract way.

In this collection more personal details of Brautigan's private life surface than in his later published works.

dear old mommie

My mother
was quite
a gal.

Yup.

God bless
her soul
that
did a perfect
imitation
of a mole.

His anger at his mother and her passivity is here as evident as his fury at his father was repressed. He mentioned to me that he had met his biological father twice, once in a barbershop and once in a hotel room, and each time his father gave him some money to go see a movie. He said this in a monotone, leaving it to his listener to imagine.

Of his childhood and adolescence he was never forthcoming during the early years that I knew him. Later, after he was successful, he occasionally talked on the subject when he was in an expansive mood, usually through good food and drink. Sometimes his stories of small-town boredom were funny, such as the time he and some pals were out late one night and came across a Great Dane. Without speaking, two of them picked up the Great Dane, carried him into a local hospital by a back door, and left him in an empty operating room. "We never talked about what we were going to do with the dog," Richard explained. "We all acted like this was the job we had to do." Mostly he recalled in general terms how rough it was as a young boy, moving from one welfare motel to another, accompanied by shifting stepfathers. He also hinted at child abuse on the part of his mother.

In "a trite story," he recalls his abandonment in a Montana hotel by his mother when he was nine or ten. I heard various versions of this episode from him. Sometimes he included his younger sister and his fears about her fate; sometimes he spoke of insomnia, staring at the hotel door and trying to magic his mother's return. Once he talked about being terrified that if he touched its white doorknob his hand would freeze to it.

Throughout his writing, images of doors and doorknobs return, often associated with terror, loss, or rapid change.

Only when Brautigan reached adolescence did his life gain some domestic stability, but he was circumspect about that because it recalled his anger toward his mother over their previous wayward and rootless life. His willpower, which was ferocious and constant (and which he probably considered his only true friend, along with his imagination), banished any memories in order for him to continue as an artist. And except for his last book, *So the Wind Won't Blow It All Away*, he only infrequently called on these Northwest memories in his art, mostly in his very short stories.

Even as a young man, Brautigan concocted characteristically homespun metaphors and similes to make some sense of a world gone strange. These tropes often simply register transformation that come without conflict or setup. In "poem 4: love poem" he writes:

> Sleeping
> with her
> is like
> sleeping
> with a
> witch's
> broom.

Woman as the enemy, woman as the enchanter gone bad, these are constant laments in his poetry, with the figure of the witch a recurring one. Fourteen or so years after his writing "poem 4: love poem," at the height of his fame, Brautigan returned to the conceit with the poem "Have you ever had a witch bloom like a highway on your mouth?"

The epigrammatic quality of this type of verse derives from several sources, most importantly *The Greek Anthology*. Brautigan spoke of his joy at discovering the anthology early in his career. In San Francisco he owned a copy of the five-volume set and would read from it in company. He delighted in its simplicity and emotional impact, such as this from Leontius: "Touch, cup, those lips which give honey, suck now while you have the chance. No envy, but a wish your luck were mine."

Like many poetic young men, Brautigan fancied himself a rebel, a pose that was reinforced by his poverty, social naiveté, and wayward imagination. The humiliation over being able to afford only one pair of cheap tennis shoes a year, he once confided, "made me spend months too embarrassed to look at my feet. I thought if I didn't notice them, others wouldn't either." He tried to fight back in verse, writing lines like "a castrated cow grazing in the peace of mental death" in a poem mawkishly titled "against conformity and averageism."

This low-key rebellion led to one of the suppressed episodes in his life, his incarceration for a few months in a mental institution. In this collection, the event is represented by two starkly minimalist prose pieces, "A Love Letter from State Insane Asylum" and "I Watched the World Glide Effortlessly Bye." In the latter, the story is told in eighty-three chapters that are either single sentences or parts of sentences. Dedicated to his friend Edna Webster, the story does not give the reasons for his being there; the background, however, is illuminating. According to William Hjortsberg, Brautigan's biographer, Richard showed his poems to a girlfriend, and when she criticized them, he was so distraught that he went to a police station and asked the police to arrest him. They said they couldn't; he hadn't done anything illegal. Brautigan then threw a rock through a glass partition in the station, which earned him his stay in the institution.

At the time these poems and stories were written, Brautigan had been living in Eugene for some years, and it is easy to see the effects of access to a good university library. Locals remember Richard as a voracious reader. Scattered throughout these works are references to and imitations of well-known writers such as T. S. Eliot, Ernest Hemingway, and Ring Lardner. Some poems reveal less obvious borrowing from Kenneth Fearing and Kenneth Patchen, chiefly in unconvincing versions of their tough, streetwise personas, which quickly dropped out of Brautigan's writing. Even at the tender age of twenty-one, Brautigan was working at his own style and vision. What awaited him in the future was the education of San Francisco life, the Beat Generation, and City Lights bookshop's stock of international literature.

That this unworldly, naive, and eccentric young man went to San Francisco and became an internationally known author remains an improbable example of the American Dream. Via his persona as author — perhaps best represented by the 1967 hippie photograph on the covers of his books — he stepped into a life of acclaim, money, beautiful women, and famous friends. As Richard, ever a committed Northwest existentialist, once wrote: "All the secrets of my past have just come my way, but I still don't know what I'm going to do next." Here are some of the secrets from Brautigan's past.

KEITH ABBOTT

Why Unknown
Poets Stay Unknown,
Part 1

My name is Richard Brautigan. I am twenty-one years old.

I am an unknown poet. That does not mean I do not have any friends. It means mostly my friends know I am a poet, because I have told them so.

Let us pretend that my mind is a taxi and suddenly ("What the hell's coming off!") you are riding in it.

For Edna,
and anybody else
who happens
to be around.

knife

Build a wall
around your heart,
so that love
can never
get in.

Love is crueler
than the knife
of a man
who slit
the throats
of four children.

the wait

It seemed
like years
before
I picked
a bouquet
of kisses
off her mouth
and put them
into a dawn-colored vase
in
my
heart.

But
the wait
was worth it.

Because
I
was
in love.

x

Money

is

sad

shit.

song of a sex deviate

I'm
Always
Chasing
Rainbows

the south

"Mommie,
how does God
keep His house warm?"

"He burns
the souls
of bad niggers."

good-bye

The melody
has ended.

The flute
will never
play again.

Put it
into a box.
Bury the box.

Stand there
and remember
the melody
of the flute.

Cry some.
   Go away.
Slowly.

(Good-bye, Mother.
Father. Somebody.
Good-bye.)

*(And the wind
of a warm
autumn afternoon
causes leaves
to scratch
against
the tombstone.)*

      Good-bye

man

Some people believe
that man
is a son-of-a-bitch.

Some people believe
that man is an angel
without wings.
(A rather morbid
thought.)

I believe both parties
are right and wrong.

I also have
a few ideas of my own.

More
        or
              less.

a woman's eyes

The pure blue ocean
of
your eyes
rises and falls gently,
rises and falls gently,
and washes
nice things
up onto the beaches
of
my soul.

(Question:
           Is
this poem
as beautiful
as two five dollar bills
rubbing together?)

i dreamt i was a bird

I
dreamt
I was a bird
sitting
in an apple tree.

The sun
was out
and my feathers
were warm.

I was
resting
between courting
sessions
when some kids
snipped me off
with a BB gun.

o life!

O life!
O beauty!
O wonderful
splendor
of everything!

(Hell, man,
take
an aspirin
before you
blow a fuse.)

poem for l.w.

Could I,
would I
give you
a sky.

Filled
with
everything
you like.

. . . and
the clouds
would be
all
the dreams
you've
wanted
to come true.

And
you would
float
on them.

television program

Shredded Cardboard,
the all-American
breakfast cereal,
presents
"New Horizons
in American
Cereal and Culture."

Tonight
our star
is
Marilyn Monroe!

dear old mommie

My mother
was quite
a gal.

Yup.

God bless
her soul
that
did a perfect
imitation
of a mole.

i discovered death

At
a
moment
in life
I discovered
that I
was going
to die.

It did not
bother me
at all.

At
another
moment
in life
I discovered
what dying meant.

I
thought
it
was a dirty deal.

ex-lovers meet

Our eyes
spit
at each other.

She said
with a voice

colder than
a dead bird
(or
was it
two dead birds?),

"Hello."

nightmare

A nightmare
came to me.

The nightmare
was wearing
a bikini
bathing suit.

Dig that
sexy horror!

a nickel

The old man
stopped the boy
on the street.

"Boy?"
*With a sort
of tired voice.*

"Yeah."
*With a sort
of scared voice.*

"Am I alive?"

"Huh?"

"I don't
know whether
I'm dead
or alive.
Will you
please tell me?"

"You're."
("*Gulp.*")
"Alive."

"That's nice
to know.
Thank you.
Here's
a nickel
for your trouble."

incongruity

I remember
a very beautiful,
quite proper
young woman
letting
a fart
that sounded
like
a gunshot.

lonny

Lonny is
two years old.

Yesterday
she and I
whispered
together.

I didn't know
what she was
whispering about,
and she didn't
know what I was
whispering about.

We whispered
very softly,
and acted as if
we understood
each other
perfectly.

a game called eternity

The simplicity
of life
and the complexity
of death
play a game
called eternity
against
the complexity
of life

and the simplicity
of death.

men

sitting
in
a puddle
of puke
was
a man.

He was crying.

I asked him
if I could help
him.

He told me
to mind my own
god-damn business.

I did
and went away.

horsemeat for sale

I
galloped
like
an
enchanted horse
into love.

portrait of man

What would
you do
if the rain
fell up?

Me?

Yeah.

Get used
to living
on a cloud,
I guess.

nothing new

There
is
nothing new
under the sun
except
you and me.

the eternal she

I gave
a girl my soul.

She looked at it.

Smiled faintly.

And dropped
it into the gutter.

Casually.

God! she had class.

a young man

Surely goodness
and mercy
shall follow me
all the days
of my life,
and I will dwell
in the house
of the Lord
forever, if the
rent isn't too high.

it's raining

The rain
has started
up its unreal city,
building
its houses
and streets
and people.

The rain
has started
up its unreal city,
quickly,
            delicately.

. . . and
a little boy
looks out
the window
and says,
"Mommie, it's raining."

But
the boy's mother
does not hear him
because
of the rain.

if i should die before you do

When
you wake up
from death,
you will find yourself
in my arms,
and
I will be
kissing you,
and
I
will be crying.

lesson

Hello
means
that
hell is low.

It is
a word
common among
earth people
who
should know.

fly caught in a spider's web

I
knew a man
who
was dying
of cancer.

He had
the patience
of a fly
caught
in a spider's web.

When
he died,
he asked,

"What time is it?"

let's walk downtown together

I'll take your hand,
which reminds me
of a cat I used to know,
and we'll start out walking.

I'll talk to you about things,
and I'll make you smile
and giggle and laugh
like a little kid.

I'll point out things for you
to look at.

Maybe I'll stop and kiss you
right out in front of everybody.

I won't give a damn either
because I love you
more than a mountain
I used to know.

breathe on me

One
of thousands of cheap rented rooms.
One
of thousands of tired, lonely people.
        She watches
        the rain write
        autumn
        on the window.

        After a few years
        she says,
        "God, please breathe on me."

        After a few more years
        she says,
        "I think
        I'll go out

and
get
a bowl of soup."

against conformity and averageism

I hate,

because
they are evil
as habitual hunger
in a child's stomach,

people
who try
to change man
the hunter for truth
into
a castrated cow
grazing
in the peace
of mental death.

maggots eating my brains

The maggots
will eat
the brains
that felt
and wondered
and wrote
these poems.

Let the maggots
have their fun.

21

They
only
live once.

gay: tra la-la

Flowers
on
the
mountain.

("My God,
they're beautiful.
It's
days like this
make you glad
to be alive, Joe."
"Yeah, Al.")

Gay: tra la-la.
Gay: tra la-la.

Summer is just a day,
but so is death.

Gay: tra la-la.

god, have mercy on this young lover

When
I am kissing
you,
I can
look down

on all things
that are wonderful.

(Destroy
him
instantly.)

all the cities at once

Pretend
is
a city
bigger
than New York,
bigger
than
all the cities
at once.

a memory of life will be frozen in my eyes

The heads
of white chickens
lie in the mud and rain.

A memory
of life
is frozen in their eyes.

I wonder
what their last thought
was
as their heads
were chopped off.

phantom kiss

There
is no worse
hell
than
to remember
vividly
a kiss
that
never occurred.

the wooer

I will woo
you carefully
as somebody
(big)
planning
to cheat
somebody
(small.)

I will woo
you
so carefully
that you
will get
so impatient
that you
will start
to woo me.

If that doesn't work,
I'll try something else.

don't be afraid of death

When you are old
and about to be eaten
by a coffin,
        don't
        be afraid
        of death.

Naa.

white tiger and enchanted cave

I am
a white tiger
made
out of peppermint.

There
is an enchanted cave
in your body
that I must enter,
so
that chills
will travel
in new buses
up
and
down
our spines
as
we stare
at our
very own baby.

the death of time

Someday
Time
will die,
and
Love
will
bury it.

The Conscripted Storyteller

"Are you a woodpecker?" I asked.

"*No,*" she said. "I'm a little girl. Where have you been lately, Mister?"

I *had* been standing in the literature section of the public library reading a book by Watson T. Smith Brownly in which he put forth, most logically, the idea that all writers and poets should stop writing and take up bricklaying instead. I had been very absorbed in the book when somebody had started tapping on my leg. It had been the first time that I had been reading a book in the library and somebody had started tapping on my leg. I had been curious. I had looked down, and there was a little girl with blond hair, a green dress, and blue eyes, tapping on my leg with her forefinger.

"Where's your mother, little girl?" I asked.

"Shopping," she said.

"What are you doing here?" I said. "And will you please stop tapping on my leg."

"My mother left me here to read while she went shopping. I've been reading a book."

"Why don't you go back and read your book?" I suggested.

"It's corny," she said.

"What am I supposed to do about it?"

"Tell me a story," she said.

"What!"

"Quiet," she said, "or you'll wake up everybody."

"I don't want to tell you a story," I said. "I want to read my book."

"You're *going* to tell me a story."

"Why me?" I said.

"Because I checked to see who has the biggest mouth here, and you've got it."

"What will you do if I refuse to tell you a story?" I asked.

"Oh, nothing," she said sweetly. "I'll just start screaming as loud as I can, and when everybody comes over here, I'll tell them you're my father. I've been told that when I scream, it sounds like the end of the world. I may even bite somebody: some nice innocent old lady. Have you ever been chained to a galley oar, Mister?"

I knew that I had had it, so I reluctantly put the book back on the shelf. "I'll tell you a story outside on the steps," I said in a tone of the vanquished.

"I *knew* you'd see it my way," she said.

I walked out of the library holding on to the small hand of a little girl who I knew, without a doubt, would disprove Einstein's theory of relativity.

I sat down on the steps of the library, and she sat down casually on my lap. I glanced over at the old, vine-covered city hall where there were pigeons standing on the roof and cooing.

"How'd you like to hear a story about a pigeon?" I asked.

"One of those pigeons?" she said, pointing at the roof of the city hall.

"Yes," I said.

"No," she said.

"Why not?" I said.

"They look like a bunch of goofs to me," she said.

"What kind of story do you want to hear, then?"

"One with a nice messy homicide in it, and very terse like Hemingway. I hate digression."

"Huh?"

"Well, hurry," she said impatiently.

"Have you heard the story about Dracula?"

"*Yes*," she said. "*That* story is as old as the Carpathians."

"How about a science-fiction story?"

"Not a space-cadet type," she said sophisticatedly.

"Once upon a time," I started, "there was a race of five-headed scorpions living on Neptune."

"How banal," she said. "That beginning is a mossback, and besides, the atmosphere on Neptune lies frozen on the ground. How could five-headed scorpions live without atmosphere, well?"

There was a long moment of silence.

"Are you sure you want to hear a story?" I asked. "Why don't you go back in the library and read Nietzsche or Jung or somebody?"

"I *want* to hear a story."

"All — all right," I said obsequiously.

I told her a story about some leopard frogs that had high intellects, and how they had discovered a way to travel in the fourth dimension, and how they would've taken over the world if they hadn't made one mistake: they went so deep in the fourth dimension that they tumbled into the fifth dimension, and they couldn't get back to the fourth dimension so they couldn't do any harm to Earth because it operates strictly on a third- and fourth-dimensional basis. When I finished the story, I had a headache.

The little girl cogitated a silent moment, with a very serious expression on her face. Then she got off my lap and said slowly, "Mister, why don't you go back in and read your book?"

I scurried like a wounded crab back into the library. I never saw the little girl again, thank God!

Would You Like to Saddle Up a Couple of Goldfish and Swim to Alaska?

.

for Edna

I

It's an old story and sort of corny.

•

Grace was seventeen.
I was nineteen.

•

We were in love.

II

Grace

The dawn was a fragile glow in the room.

•

I lay awake and watched the day bloom, and I stared at Grace who was sound asleep.

•

The peaceful warm of her body was close up against me.

•

There was a dim memory of lipstick on her mouth.

•

Her breathing was slow and heavy with sleep.

•

Grace was more beautiful than anything that I have ever seen.

•

"I love you," I whispered.

•

And stroked gently her brown hair.

Grace

    I was writing a short story and listening to the rain come down outside and wondering when Grace was going to get back from town.

•

    Suddenly Grace was there.

•

    She was dripping wet.
Her hair and everything.

•

    She was laughing.

•

    "What's so funny?" I asked.

•

    "Nothing, honey," she said.

•

    "Then why are you laughing?"

•

    "I'm soaking wet!"

•

    Her voice was as excited and happy as a child playing in a hayloft.

Grace

    I liked to watch Grace eat.

•

    I liked to watch Grace eat because she ate poetically.

•

    I mean . . .

•

    Well . . .

•

    I have never known anyone else who ate poetically.

Grace

　　I remember the roses that grew next to the pond.

　　●

　　They were red as a baby's blood.

　　●

　　I remember Grace picking one of the roses and putting it
in her hair and looking at me with her blue eyes and saying,
"Did you ever want to be a rose?"

Grace

　　I went into the bathroom and Grace was there taking
a bath.

　　●

　　"Hi, honey," she said.

　　●

　　"Taking a bath?"

　　●

　　"Uh-huh."

　　●

　　She was rubbing soap all over breasts and chest and
stomach.

　　●

　　I unbuckled my pants and pulled them down.

　　●

　　I took down my shorts, sat on the toilet and tried to
defecate.

　　●

　　It was very nice and pure knowing a girl as well as I knew
myself.

III

Grace

I cannot say to the one I love, "Hi, flower-wonderful bird-love sweet."

•

Watcha doin? If you're like me, you're doin nothin, but you're doin it so well that everybody thinks you're doin somethin.

•

I cannot say to the one I love, "Besides being the world's greatest unknown writer, I play a fair game of kick the can."

•

I cannot say to the one I love, "Want to go to a cave and eat some popcorn, or would you like to saddle up a couple of goldfish and swim to Alaska?"

•

I cannot say.

•

I cannot do.

•

Or anything.

•

Because Grace is full of embalming fluid.

•

And she is lying in the cold darkness of a box.

•

Six feet under the ground.

IV

Grace

"Come here," I said.

•

"Yes, master," Grace said.

•

We laughed.

•

Grace walked slowly towards me, and then she was in my arms where she fitted like a key.

•

"What do you want?" she whispered.

•

I could barely hear her voice.

•

"Why are you so beautiful?" I asked.

•

Grace giggled.

V

. . . and they lived happily ever after.

The Egg Hunter

She was rainin pretty hard. Big drops of rain. Big like strawber-
ries comin quicklike down out of the sky that black like my dog
Sam. And there was a wind blowin the rain sort of sideways
against the yella grass. The grass was belly high and all wet. It
was sure a hellofa day to be in the grass. I was all soaked clear to
the skin right through my pants and my shirt and my shoes felt
all squishy. I weren't wearin a hat and my face and my hair was
all wet just like I took a bath or went swimmin. I was lookin
pretty hard along the top of the hill when it started rainin. I
didnt think it was gonna rain when I started lookin but I guess I
was wrong. I aint usually wrong about the weather so much so I
was pretty surprised when it started rainin I mean it was almost
the first time I was wrong. So I had to give up lookin for squirrel
eggs and get the hell down to the crick where them big trees are.
It was sure rainin and walkin down through that yella grass was
sure pretty wet gettin. I was sure glad when I got down to the
crick and them trees. I crawled under the low branches of one of
them trees and it was just like bein in a cave but it didnt smell
wavelike it smelled clean. It sure felt good to get out of the rain
because she was so bad. I sat there all drippin and dry dust
under the tree stuck to my clothes. The rain and wind was
makin a funny sound in the upstairs of the trees. Sort of a scared
sound. I sure didnt like it too much. I don't know how long I sat
there under the tree when I heard sounds comin. They was people I couldnt hardly hear them because the rain and wind was so
loud. They got closer and closer and I could hear them pretty
good. They was Ben and Sally who cooks food over at my uncle
Lems house. She wears red lips and she sticks out in front like
shes got watermelons under her dress. They was holdin hands. I
didnt make no sounds. I don't like Ben he kicked me one day
and he made my front teeth fall out and my mouth all bloody
and it hurt like hell for along time. I didnt make no noise. I just
layed there awful quietlike like I was an old dead chicken. And
they walked right by me and they didnt see me. I was sure glad.

They stopped aways away from me and they got down under a tree and Ben started to kiss Sally all over her face and her red lips. He stuck his hand way down in her dress and he unbuttoned his pants like he had to go number one. He did somethin I couldnt hardly believe at all I mean they was just like sheep and dogs and cows and things. I watched them do it. It sure made me feel pretty funny all over. The rain stopped comin down and I crawled quietlike out from under the tree and into the wet grass until I was an awful ways away from Ben and Sally. It was sure pretty wet gettin. I did it quietlike. A guys got to be careful around Ben. Bens mean he kicked me and he makes fun at me. He says Im stupider then a drunk dog. Sometimes Im slow all right but it aint my fault. I try awful hard. Im bigger then Ben. Id hurt Ben if he wasnt so mean. I got back up to the hill where my brother Charley says theres squirrel eggs. I looked under the rocks for the eggs. I looked in the grass and gopher holes and bushes and just everywhere all afternoon untill things started to get dark. But I guess I didnt look good enough because I didnt find no squirrel eggs. Not even one.

James Dean in Eugene, Oregon

I met Bob in Tiffany-Davis on Willamette Street. I had not seen Bob for five years. We had gone to Woodrow Wilson Junior High School together.

We stood in front of the magazine rack and talked and smiled a lot as guys do when they have not seen each other for a long time.

"Want a Coke or something to drink?" Bob said after a few moments.

"Sure," I said.

We went back to the fountain and sat down. A waitress came over. Bob asked me what I wanted. "I think I'll have a Coke," I said. Bob ordered a cup of coffee.

We sat there and talked about days gone forever from the earth, and how things looked a lot different when you're twenty years old. We talked about all sorts of things.

Then Bob mentioned that he had wanted to be an actor and had fooled around in Hollywood for a while and had met some actors. Bob told me that he had met James Dean in Schwab's drugstore at Hollywood and Vine.

I had seen James Dean in *East of Eden* and thought that he was a very sensitive actor. But like most of the movie stars, James Dean seemed very unreal to me. He belonged to a world that reminded me of a big fairy tale. I had always thought of movie stars as sort of imitation people.

"Dean wears glasses," Bob said, "thick glasses."

"Huh," I said.

"I was with some other guys," Bob said. "We sat there and talked, but Dean didn't say much. He doesn't say much at all. Just listens most of the time, but when he says something, he says *something*. He's very intelligent, but awfully quiet. He doesn't ramble on about nothing. When he says something, he says *something*. You know what I mean?"

40

"Sure, I know."

I could tell by the expression in Bob's voice that he liked James Dean. Bob talked about James Dean for just a moment, but when he had finished, I felt as if I had met James Dean, too. And he seemed very real to me, and I liked him. It was a strange, nice feeling.

This all occurred one afternoon in Eugene, Oregon, before James Dean was killed.

A Love Letter from
State Insane Asylum

A

Calvin
was
three years old.

1

The graveyard was a quiet place.
•
It was quieter than any other place I had ever been to.
•
Even church.
•
There were tall, tall trees all around the graveyard.
•
A wind blew through the trees and made them talk with lovely voices.
•
The grass was so green.
•
There was a strange feeling all around the graveyard.
•
It was a perfect place for dead people to live.

2

The rain was just pouring down on the other side of the window.
•
I pressed my face against the window.
•
The window was cold.
•

I saw the lights of a car come up the road.

•

I thought it was Uncle Ray.

•

But it wasn't.

3

We went on a picnic way back into the woods.

•

It was a lot of fun.

•

I found a flower.

•

A blue one.

4

Once I reached for a biscuit.

•

My daddy was mad.

•

He hit my hand with his fork.

•

That made me cry.

5

I went down to the beach and sat in the light sand.

•

The biggest water in the whole world came up the dark sand and stopped about five feet away from me.

•

Then the water slid back down again.

•

The water kept doing that over and over and over.

•

The water made me happy.

6

I had a yellow cat whose name was Tom.

•

He purred a lot and was a pretty nice cat.

•

I loved him so much.

•

One day he went away.

•

He never came back home again.

7

The wind started to flow and the house started to creak.

•

And creak. And creak.

•

I got scared.

•

I thought the house was waking up.

8

I got a hold of a spider.

•

He squirmed in my hands.

•

"I won't hurt you," I said.

•

But the spider kept on squirming.

•

He was a big black spider.

•

Mommie came in and yelled, "DROP that spider!"

•

"I'm not hurting him," I said.

9

"You're so beautiful," my mommie said.

•

"You're just a little fairy doll."

•

She held me in her arms, and she kept kissing me.

•

I touched one of the little hills on her front.

•

It was soft.

•

There were two of them.

•

I loved them both like I loved my mommie's eyes and her voice.

•

My mommie had a mouth that tasted better than peanut butter.

10

Some sunlight came in through the window.
-
In the sunlight pieces of dust moved around and around.
-
I didn't know they were dust.
-
I thought they were baby bugs.
-
I tried hard to catch one of them.
-
But I never could.

Z

Calvin
was
twenty years old.

Dear Jane,

My parents came here, and they told me things. They told me what things people said to the police about me. Oh God, Jane, you were so right when you said that no one would understand me. To them, I am a monster. A monster. A monster.

•

I wonder if the police questioned Estella about me. Today I asked my parents to call you up and find out. Was that wrong? Tomorrow they will tell me. Tomorrow. Tomorrow. I know that I can never try to enchant Estella if they have questioned her about me.

•

You know how much I love her. You know how deep and pure and true my love is. I cannot live without Estella. Without her, I will just exist.

•

Why did I have to meet Estella? Why did I fall in love with her? Why? Why? Why? Why am I everlastingly in love with someone I have one chance in a million of getting? What evil have I done to deserve so much horror? Pray for me, Jane. Pray that God will have mercy on my soul. Please pray for me.

•

I love you very much, Jane. You are the only person who understands me. You are the only person who knows what I am: a confused little rabbit in a jungle full of tigers.

•

I want to write. I want to write and write and write. I want to obtain money so that I can give nice things to Estella. I want with all my soul to give Estella the beautiful things that a beautiful girl like her should have. I doubt if I will ever have the chance to enchant Estella, but I hope and pray that I can at least give her nice things that will make her happy even if I can't make her happy myself. All I want out of life is to make Estella happy, to protect her against the jungle, and take care of her for always. For God's sake, Jane, is that too much to ask? Is that greed? Jane, I can't live for myself. I have to live for somebody. Please ask God to have mercy on my soul.

•

Every night I pray for Estella. I pray that she will have a wonderful life and be spared from nightmares. I pray that God will protect her, and watch over her, and guide her down the path of Good. I hope with all my soul that God will answer my prayers.

•

And along comes a gentle hunter armed only with a rose.

Yours,
Calvin

I Watched the World Glide Effortlessly Bye

We were all little children.

Book One

chapter 1
> Once

chapter 2
> upon a time I was a little boy

chapter 3
> in love with a brown teddy bear.

chapter 4
> Then

chapter 5
> I was eighteen years old

chapter 6
> and I was sitting in a room in the Lane County Courthouse.

chapter 7
> There were some men in the room.

chapter 8
> The men

chapter 9
> told me that they were committing me

chapter 10
> to the State Insane Asylum.

chapter 11
> Then I was standing outside the room.

chapter 12
I remember my mother coming

chapter 13
dream-like

chapter 14
towards me,

chapter 15
and she was crying.

chapter 16
Her lips formed the word Tommy,

chapter 17
but no sound came from them

chapter 18
except crying.

chapter 19
My father said,

chapter 20
"Everything is going to be O.K."

chapter 21
"Yes," I said.

chapter 22
"They're sending me away

chapter 23
to the madhouse.

chapter 24
    Everything

chapter 25
    is going to be all right.

chapter 26
    You bet."

Book Two

chapter 1
    . . . and

chapter 2
    I was in the front seat of a car.

chapter 3
    A guard

chapter 4
    was sitting beside me.

chapter 5
    The car

chapter 6
    left my hometown, Eugene, Oregon,

chapter 7
    and started towards Salem,

chapter 8
    where the State Insane Asylum is located.

chapter 9
    It was raining.

chapter 10
   The rain came gently from a gray winter sky.

chapter 11
   Jesus Christ

chapter 12
  was sitting in the back seat.

chapter 13
   He had on a pair of handcuffs.

chapter 14
   A guard

chapter 15
   was sitting beside him.

chapter 16
   "God, why did you take our mother away?"

chapter 17
   Jesus Christ said.

chapter 18
   "God, why did you take our mother away?"

chapter 19
   Jesus Christ said.

chapter 20
   Jesus Christ had a face mild as a lamb's.

chapter 21
   He moved and his handcuffs jingled.

chapter 22
>He did not move again

chapter 23
>for a long time.

chapter 24
>He did not say anything again

chapter 25
>for a long time.

chapter 26
>I stared out the window.

chapter 27
>"It's rainin'," said the guard in the back seat.

chapter 28
>"Yeah," said the guard in the front seat.

chapter 29
>They had guard-like voices.

chapter 30
>The windshield wiper

chapter 31
>went back and forth,

chapter 32
>back and forth,

chapter 33
>back and forth,

chapter 34
back and forth.

chapter 35
"God, not our mother!" yelled Jesus Christ.

chapter 36
"Not our mother!"

chapter 37
"Shut that up!"

chapter 38
said the guard in the back seat.

chapter 39
Jesus Christ did not say anything else

chapter 40
for a long time.

chapter 41
And neither did the guards.

chapter 42
I listened to the windshield wiper

chapter 43
and stared out the window

chapter 44
and thought about the girl whom I loved.

chapter 45
I could see her face, hear her voice.

chapter 46
  I could imagine

chapter 47
  what she thought

chapter 48
  about me being taken away

chapter 49
  to the State Insane Asylum.

chapter 50
  I tried very hard not to cry.

chapter 51
  I stared out the window.

chapter 52
  I saw a little boy

chapter 53
  sitting on the front porch of an old house.

chapter 54
  The little boy was holding a white cat in his arms.

chapter 55
  I tried very hard not to cry.

chapter 56
  I stared out the window

chapter 57
  and watched the world glide effortlessly bye.

Somebody from Hemingway Land

They were sitting at a table in a bar which was inhabited by smart-looking people who were drinking and laughing and having a lot of fun.

"Anyway," she said, "that's it. You're not fun anymore, and I don't want to see you again. You were —"

"That's awfully damn nice," Art said, staring at her for a few seconds and then he looked back down at the table again.

"Don't start talking like somebody from Hemingway Land," she said. "Can't you just let it drop instead, instead of being a melodramatic ass."

His face finished getting white. His mouth was trembling slightly.

"I can't stand puerile scenes," she said. "Infantilism. Infantilesism."

A tall waiter came over and asked them if they wanted to order now.

"Hell, no," Art said, without looking up from the table.

The waiter walked very slowly away. He had been a prizefighter once.

"I'm leaving," she said.

"Go on," he said. "Go on."

She got up from the table.

"Goodbye."

"Beat it," he said. He stared at the table and listened to her walk away. When he looked up she was gone.

The people at the next table were laughing so loudly that he could not hear his brain.

"The damn nigger bitch," he said. Then he started crying.

There's Always Somebody
Who Is Enchanted

maybe this is the way the world will end

"Sure. Sure. Sure. Sure. Sure. Sure. Sure," he said.

•

"'Sure,'" I said, "'Sure, sure.' Is that all you can say?"

•

"Sure."

•

I really didn't mean to kill my husband with that ax.

•

But he made me so mad.

mr. allen

I remember the afternoon that eighty-year-old Mr. Allen was evicted from his room.

•

They took his clothes and furniture and things, and they piled them out on the sidewalk.

•

Mr. Allen did not know what it was all about.

•

He sat there in his rocking chair for over two hours.

•

It was raining, and all his things got wet.

monsters that drink human blood

The autumn night was very dark. A cold wind blew through the city, and the wind shook the trees and it stirred the leaves and made the power lines talk like angry ghosts.

•

Geese were flying on the night, and every once in a while a flock could be heard passing over the city.

•

Two nine-year-old boys were walking down a street. It was after midnight and they had just seen a horror move, *The Thing.*

•

The boys were holding hands.

•

"What do you think?" Gary asked.

"I don't want to meet any monsters that drink human blood," Jim said.

•

"Neither do I."

"Do you want to run some?"

"Just for exercise," Gary said.

•

"Sure."

They ran like hell down the street.

•

They ran until their sides hurt, and they had to stop. They didn't say anything for a moment. They just stood there and panted.

•

A flock of geese passed overhead. The geese were flying very low.

"I wonder if these geese are dangerous," Gary said.

"I don't know, but I sure hope not."

"What would you do if a flock of geese swooped down and tried to take us away?" Gary said.

•

"Gods!" Jim said.

there's always somebody who is enchanted

"What are you thinking about?" Kim asked. "You look like you're a million miles away."

"Do girls really have to go to the toilet?" I said.

•

When I was in my early teens, it seemed awfully vulgar to me that girls had to go to the toilet.

•

"You're crazy!" Kim said.

•

She was sitting on my knee.
She started laughing, and she laughed pretty hard for quite a time.

•

I couldn't see what was so funny.

awakening

The dog had fallen from a high cliff down onto the road, and then trucks and cars had run over it, I guess, because the dog was only an inch thick.

•

The dog was white, and its guts were white.

•

When I saw the dog I couldn't believe it for a moment.

•

Then I had to believe it.

•

Then I started crying.

•

I was five years old.
The dog was the first dead animal I had ever seen.

•

I had always thought that everything lived forever.

just love

Billie took the cap off the salt shaker and she poured the salt out on the table.

•

She spread the salt out and she wrote "John" in the salt, and she made a plus sign, then she wrote below it "Billie" in the salt.

●

Billie looked up at me and smiled.

●

I reached over and took her hand and pulled it across the table. And I kissed her hand.

trite story

I spent a winter in Butte, Montana.

●

That was after my mother had run off with a man named Frank, or Jack.

●

My father was a cook and worked long hours. I seldom saw my father, except when I ate my meals, because he was living with a whore named Virginia.

●

Virginia didn't like me.

●

I had my own hotel room.

the old women

"How's your daughter?"
"She's O.K."
"That's good. She isn't having any more trouble with her husband, is she?"

●

"No. He started acting like a lamb the minute she got pregnant. He's the best husband in the world now. Never argues with her anymore about anything. And he waits on her hand and foot."

"Oh, that's good. That's very good. I'm glad all the trouble is over."

"So am I. It was sure a mess for awhile. It's all over now, though. Everything's O.K."

"That's good."

•

"How's your back?"
"That isn't so good."
"Ohhhh. Tell me about it, dear."

•

"Well . . ."

the forest

Suddenly, I wasn't asleep anymore for I could hear the sound of the creek that was flowing about twenty feet away, and I could hear the chirping of birds.

•

I lay in my sleeping bag for awhile without opening my eyes.

•

I just lay there and listened to every sound that my ears could pick up.

•

When I finally opened my eyes the colors of the dawn were thrust into them, and for an instant the forest seemed unreal, and then it was real as anything.

a visit from jake

I laid in bed for a couple of hours trying like crazy to get to sleep, but I got nowhere, like a drunk snail.

After awhile I got pretty damn mad. I slammed my eyes shut hard as I could, and starting countin sheep.

69

I must have counted fifty thousand of the bastards.
I gave up when they started countin me.

  •

It was about three in the morning when the ghost of my
brother Jake came and visited me.

  •

I was layin there wonderin if some bright guy had ever
thought about countin naked women when in walked Jake's
ghost.

  •

Jake had been dead for about six years. I was sort of
surprised to see him.

  •

Jake looked just about like anyone else except he glowed and
I could see right through him.

  •

"Hello," Jake said.
"It's been a long time," I said.
We shook hands.

  •

Jake sat down on the bed. "You're looking swell," he said.
"Just swell."
"You're looking O.K., too," I said, "but I can see right
through you."
"That's the way it goes when you're dead," Jake said.

  •

We sat there and talked for awhile about a whole mess of
things.
We had a lot to talk about.

  •

After awhile we got up from the bed and went into the
kitchen, and got a couple cans of beer out of the icebox.
Me and Jake sat there in the kitchen and drank beer and
talked some more.

  •

It was sure nice seein Jake again.

70

You just don't really appreciate people until after they've been dead for a few years.

rock around the clock

He was in a booth playing "Rock Around the Clock" when she came into the record store.

•

She was wearing a gray coat and white shoes. She was fifteen years old and pretty. She walked over to the table where the popular records were kept and started to look at them.

•

He stared at her through the glass door of the booth.
He stared intensely at her.
His mouth got wet.

•

Suddenly she looked up and saw him staring at her. She stared at him for a few seconds, and then she looked back down at the records.

•

He continued to stare at her.

•

She could feel him staring at her.

•

It caused her to get excited, but she didn't show it.

•

She tried very hard not to show it.

•

She selected two records and walked over to the empty booth that was next to his.

•

The booth had glass walls. She opened the door and went in. She put "Love is a Many-Splendored Thing" on the phonograph.

•

He glanced at her.

•

She glanced at him.

•

They kept glancing at each other.

•

Then he stopped the phonograph, took "Rock Around the Clock" off the turntable and left the booth.

•

He stepped over to her booth, and he stared at her through the door.
She stared back.

•

He knocked gently on the door.
She opened it.
"Hi," he said.
"Hi," she said.

•

"I like you," he said. "What's your name?"
"Pat."

The Flower Burner

Penny didn't show up and I felt awfully bad about it. I mean —
well, I was counting on it, but she didn't show up and I felt
awfully bad about it. Penny usually comes down to the crick in
the middle of the afternoon and she swims naked for a couple of
minutes, but she didn't show up yesterday.

I sure like to hide in the bushes and watch Penny swim
naked, because she's just about the prettiest Indian in the whole
county. I sure felt bad yesterday when she didn't show up. I
waited in the bushes for over an hour, then I knew she wasn't
coming and so I decided to go home and do something. I
crawled out of the bushes and went up through the fir trees to
the road and started home.

Yesterday was sure a hot day. Hotter than hell on Saturday
night, I guess.

I was walking along when Mr. Perlich came riding down the
road on his horse. He stopped beside me.

"Howdy, Mr. Perlich," I said.

"Hot ain't it?" he said.

"Yeah. Sort of."

Mr. Perlich is a tall, skinny guy with no hair. He hasn't got a
hair on his head. All his hair dropped out the day after his wife
blew her head off with a shotgun.

"You know what?" Mr. Perlich said.

"What?"

"Oh. Oh, I don't know," he said. Then he rode off without so
much as saying another word. Mr. Perlich always does things
like that. He's been doing them ever since his wife blew her
head off.

Mr. Perlich went around a bend in the road and I couldn't see
him anymore. I started walking again.

It was sure hot and I was sweating awfully bad. My knees felt
sort of weak, because I didn't have much for lunch.

I saw a big, fat rattlesnake sunning himself on the front porch
of Winston's tumble-down old cider mill. I threw a rock at the

snake, but I missed him and he rattled and scurried under the steps. I could see him peeking out at me. I threw another rock and he crawled back under the mill and I couldn't see him anymore. I sure bet he was mad!

There was one cloud in the sky above the cider mill. It was a white cloud shaped just like a cuspidor. You don't see too many clouds these days that look like cuspidors.

When I passed by the Hinshaws' place, I saw Ben Hinshaw sitting on a branch in the top of the big maple tree that's in front of the house. Ben Hinshaw is 64 years old and he's got a face that looks like a monkey's. He was peeking at me from behind a leaf.

"What in the hell are you doing up there?" I yelled.

"Go way," he said.

"What's wrong with you?"

"Go way. Go way. I'm a bird. Leave me alone. Go way."

"Oh. You're a bird, huh?"

"Yup. I'm a bird."

"What kind of bird are you?"

"A robin."

"How does it feel to be a robin?"

"Pretty good."

"That's nice."

Mrs. Hinshaw came out on the front porch of the house and yelled, "You leave him alone! You leave my husband alone! Go away and leave him alone!"

"I wasn't bothering him."

"You leave him alone and get the hell out of here."

"This is a free road," I said.

Mrs. Hinshaw sat down on the front steps and she covered up her face with her apron and she started crying. "Leave him alone. For God's sake," she said. Her voice was muffled by the apron and I could hardly hear it. "Please leave him alone."

"Okay," I said. "I'm going. You don't have to cry. Please don't cry."

"Please," she said.

I started up the road.

Ben laughed. "I'm a bird!" he yelled. "A robin!"

Mrs. Hinshaw started crying all the harder. I got the hell out of there, because when Mrs. Hinshaw cries, it makes me nervous.

I stopped only once the rest of the way home. That was to watch Mrs. Dragoo burn flowers. A couple of times a week she burns flowers. Mostly irises. She takes them and puts them in a pile and she pours kerosene on them and burns them. Then she sits down in a wicker chair beside the burning flowers and she reads her big, black Bible. Mrs. Dragoo is awfully religious. She's only missed one church service in the last 40 years. That was when the church burned down 3 years ago. Mrs. Dragoo is always reading her Bible, but, then, she's a rich widow woman and she hasn't got anything better to do. Personally, I can't stand the Bible. It's too dry. I like Mickey Spillane.

I stood there in the road and watched Mrs. Dragoo burn flowers. I can't figure out why she likes to burn flowers. Once I asked my mother about it and she said, "So what."

Suddenly Mrs. Dragoo looked up from her Bible and she stared at me for what seemed like a long while and she didn't say a word. Just stared.

"Good afternoon, Mrs. Dragoo," I said.

"You're going to hell," she said.

"Huh?"

"You heard me, young man. You're going to hell and you know it. You're going to burn forever and forever. At least a month."

"That — that isn't a very nice thing to say."

"Don't be impertinet," she said, picking up a purple iris and throwing it on the fire. "Don't be impertinet."

I shrugged my shoulders and walked home.

Some awfully weird people live in our town. Sometimes I don't know what to think.

Three Experimental Dramas

Please Let Me Walk

The curtain goes up. The stage is void of scenery. A young woman is sitting on the floor. She is wearing a plain gray dress and she does not have any shoes on. She has long hair which is disheveled and in her face.

"Once I wrote a poem," she says. "Or did I write a poem? I wonder if I wrote any poems at all. Well, anyway, I wrote a poem."

She quotes very slowly a poem:

"World with a Broken Neck

Maybe
someday
a very beautiful god
will come along
and take the world's
ugly, slimy neck
in his hands
(which will be like
the smell of roses)
and he will break
the world's neck
(SNAP!)
And afterwards
there will be no pain
or horror.
There will be only
happiness
and cities
made out of
true love
gentle as
cotton candy."

Four women come out onto the stage. They are wearing white nurse's uniforms.

They walk over to the girl and pick her up. She does not resist them. They start carrying her across the stage.

"Where are you taking me?" the girl asks weakly.

"We're going to help you," one of the women says.

"I wish you'd let me walk," the girl says.

"We're going to help you," another one of the women says.

"I wish you'd let me walk," the girl says.

"Shut up!" one of the women says sternly.

They carry the girl off the stage, and then the curtain goes down.

Everybody and the Rose

The curtain goes up. The stage is void of scenery. There is a large group of people on stage. The people are of many ages and segments of society. The people are standing perfectly still. They make no sounds. They stand there as if frozen.

An old woman comes on stage. She is carrying a bunch of roses. She tries to sell the roses to the people.

"Would you like to buy some beautiful roses?" she asks in a tired voice. She asks it over and over again to various people.

Nobody says anything.

Everybody stands perfectly still.

Finally the old woman gives up trying to sell the roses.

She starts crying.

She buries her face in the roses and continues to cry.

The curtain descends slowly.

Linda

The curtain goes up. The stage is void of scenery. A young man is pacing rapidly back and forth across the stage. He paces back and forth a few times and then he stops abruptly and stands there and rubs his hands up and down his face, and then he walks slowly over to an imaginary dresser, opens it and takes out an imaginary pistol. He points the pistol at his side.

He says softly, "Linda . . ."

He pulls the trigger of the imaginary pistol and a gunshot is heard.

He drops the pistol and the sound of a pistol hitting the floor is heard.

He falls down onto the floor. He lies there and does not move.

A young man and woman come out onto the stage. They are holding hands and laughing. They walk across the stage and stop beside the body.

They act as if it is not even there.

They kiss.

The girl says, "Isn't life wonderful?"

"It sure is!" the man says.

They walk hand-in-hand across the stage and into the wings. A burst of laughter is heard from the wings, and then the curtain goes down.

Why Unknown
Poets Stay Unknown,
Part 2

Always the Geese

Today
geese haunted the gray
of the October sky
with their V
and their eternal voices.

What can I say
that the geese didn't say
as they flew in skies far away
from the places where they were born
and grew up?

Love Is

Love is a hungry lion
eating
a
deer.

Love is a white lamb
standing in soft spring rain
and eating baby grass.

Love is a god-damn poet
writing "Love is . . ."
and knowing all the time
that love is,
and there isn't much
that he can say about it
that hasn't
been said before
by
somebody else.

But still he writes,
"Love is . . ."

Tom's Soul

All Tom's soul, a frightened, lonely, sad thing,
ever wanted was love. It only wanted a woman
to take it in her arms, and hug it, and kiss it,
and caress it, until all memories of darkness were gone,
and it knew only hugging,
and kissing,
and caressing,
until it knew only love.

But a woman did not take Tom's soul and give it love.
So,
of course, it died of thirst.

Cats

I love cats.
Why do I love cats?
I don't know exactly,
but I think it is for the same reason
that I love the dawn,
and the sunrise,
and
the coming down of rain.

Somebody Comes to This Place

It is an old story.
Somebody comes to this place
and grows up in the shadows of buildings
and stars and other somebodies.

Somebody learns to love:
to know intimately the houses
of the spirit and the flesh.

Somebody learns to hate and kill
and scream and curse like hell.

Somebody learns to be afraid and lonely
and sad, and to know the secret
of darkness.

Somebody learns to like the rain,
and things which are soft and green,
and hot food and cold water,
and the blanket of sleep,
and the music of the land and the sky.

Somebody learns so many things.

It is an old story.

Somebody comes to this place . . .
and lives . . .
and then goes away forever.

A Lonely Wet

Today
the autumn rain
was
a lovely wet.

Falling.
Falling.
Falling.

And painting
the house
of my soul
sad.

Today
the autumn rain
made
the old people
seem
very, very old.

The Haunted Heart

Life's greatest tragedy
is the haunted heart. In which
a huge love presides. A love
that cannot be resolved,
that cannot find the meaning of a kiss,
the peace of an embrace.

Always there is a man who loves a woman
that does not love him.

The shutters of the haunted heart bang, the floors
creak, and the sound of crying comes from a dark room.

In the Days of the Swans

I
remember being a child
in
a park

where there was a lake
that floated
beautiful white swans
on
    dark water.

I
remember sitting along the shore
with
childhood fantasies
flying around
like butterflies in my brain.

I
remember wishing that I were
a beautiful white swan
floating
on
    dark water.

When My Soul Didn't Love Me

Once upon a sad weird
there lived a girl
who was my beautiful soul given form.
So,
of course,
I loved her a cash-registerful.
But she didn't love me a penny.
It was very sad and weird having my soul
not love me.

A Butcher Knife

"Bring on tomorrow!
Bring her on!
Bring her on!"
yelled a man drunk with life.

Tomorrow
came and cut
his throat with a butcher knife.

Voice from a Long-Ago Dusk

I remember
a young woman's
pigeon-beautiful voice
dancing lightly
out of a June dusk
and saying,
"Life is O.K.
if you don't take
it too seriously."

Hurry, Young Lovers

Hurry, young lovers
and love while you can.

Kiss and caress
and love while you can.

Taste and devour
and love while you can.

Because soon death
will blow your fire out.

And only ashes will remain.

The Gentle Hunter

Yes,
    I, too,
have hunted for love
in the valley of the heart.

Yes,
    I, too,
have gone home empty-handed,
sometimes crying,
sometimes just staring
straight ahead,
                        but seeing nothing.

Something

There is something in me
that finds peace only when it
is in the forest, only when it
is walking on the floor of the forest
and is surrounded by trees.

Will My Soul Walk in the Rain?

Tomorrow morning
warm spring rain
will fall on my grave.

Will my soul be under the ground and asleep?
Or will it be out walking in the warm spring rain?

Tomorrow morning
I will find out.

Anyone for Kleenex?

My love
is
a beautiful bird
way up in the blue sky.

I'll never catch my love
no matter how hard I try.

**Poem for Linda Webster When She Is Old
Enough to Find Her Way Around in the
Valley of Poetry**

Linda, be kind to flowers
and stars and rivers.
Never tell lies to apples or rainbows.
Trust bread and jam and glasses
of ice-cold milk.
Give a full heart of love
to pigeons and slugs.

Always remember
that people are people
and forgive them for it . . .
and love them for it . . .

If you do these things, Linda,
you needn't be afraid of death,
for you will never die.

Days

I have lived in the days of tigers.
I have seen hot blood
dripping
off their fangs.

I have lived in the days of flowers.
I have seen smiles
dripping
off their peace.

the unemployed dreamers

I pity
people
who are not
employed
at dreaming.

poem for edna

Could I,
would I
give you a sky.

Oh, filled
with such things
as blues
sweeter than candy.

Untitled

Jesus:
    purer
    than
    the love
    of a mother cat
    for
        her kittens.

portrait of an american teenage girl

The only thing
she's good for
is a one night stand
in a motel.

And the clouds
would be all
the white dreams
you've wanted
to come true.

And you would float
on them.

farewell to my oedipus complex

For Christmas
I
will give my mother
a
time bomb.

Untitled

I
am waiting anxiously
for Hollywood to buy this book
and pay umpity-ump cash for it
and turn it into a super-colossal
spectacle with ten thousand extras;
2,000 horses, 52 lions, 60 king cobras,
and every Hollywood actress who has been
divorced over five times.

Hollywood will,
of course,
change the title
to something like

"The Outcasts of Devil's Island."

a green neon sign which is happy

Spring
is wonderful,
            (just)
and
like, perhaps,
maybe even
double perhaps,
a green neon sign
which
is happy
because
it knows it will
keep going on
and off

forever.

a hard day's work

I came home
from Muse.

My wife said,
"Did you have
a hard day
writing poems,
honey?"

"I sure did," I said.
"I'm pooped."

"That's too bad, honey,"
my wife said,
and then she started
to frighten
the tiredness
away
with gentleness.

we had fried rainbow trout for breakfast

We had
fried rainbow trout
for breakfast,
and somewhere
along the line
she kissed me
and I asked her why,
and she told me
she didn't know why,
except that she
loved me.

the mind is the strangest city

For
my birthday
I want
a dead mouse
and a blue piece of
red candy.

the unknown dreamer

Someday
I believe
(and soon)
we should erect
a fragile monument
for the Unknown Dreamer
because
he was more important
than soldiers.

of course, we will not live happily ever after

To put it bluntly,
I want to kiss you
so gently
that you will feel
towards me
for the first time
love's paralysis.

(Of course, we will not
live happily ever after,
but only
in the fashion
of human beings)

creation of a poem

A delicate bird
hit against
night's cruel beauty
and promptly laid
an enchanted egg.

there was a wire screen between us

I could have
just died,
no kidding,
when my girlfriend
came to visit me
for the first time
while I was in jail.

I was wearing
a white uniform.

There was a wire screen
between us.

"Hi," Carol said,
and she smiled
weak as water.

I could have
just died.

a coke

i remember You
drinking a coke.

i had never known
that somebody
drinking a coke
could be a beautiful poem.

the poetry of Your hands

i want to feel
the soothing poetry
of Your hands
drifting on my face.

eyes

Your
eyes
are
trout.

perhaps

boy!
love
is something.
it
is like,
perhaps,
a piece
of apple pie.

**i would walk back
across hell
to get Your hat**

i would
carry You across hell,
and
if You had forgotten
Your hat,
    i would walk
    back across hell
    and get it for You.

photograph 15

Lovers
lying
in a bed,
covered by
a sheet
with only
their feet
sticking out,
entangled.

story 3: the embarrassed hearse driver

She insisted on having the abortion. I said that I would marry
her and everything would be all right, but she insisted on having the abortion. She was seventeen years old and did not want
to have any children yet. I cried for an hour one evening, but she
insisted on having the abortion. I told her that it might kill her.
She smiled gently and said that she loved me, and that the abortion would not kill her. "Silly boy," she said.
    The whole business was ridiculous.

The hearse that took her body to the cemetery had a flat tire. I asked the hearse driver if he needed any help fixing the tire.

"This has never happened before," he said. "This has never happened before." His face was almost as red as blood.

I told her not to have the abortion. I told her.

still life 4

A brush,
a pallet,
a naked
canvas,
and a friendly
medium-sized
hallucination.

still life 1

A set
of miniature false
teeth
sitting
on the seat
of a red
tricycle.

question 4

Do
castrated
men
ever
dream
about
women?

profound saying 4

People who
live in glass
houses
have Chihuahuas
instead of
children.

photograph 12

A twelve-year-old
girl's
virtue
sitting next
to a double bed
and wondering
what
the hell happened.

family portrait 3

Six flies
standing
on a turd.

photograph 9

The first
star
in the night
sky
out of breath

but happy
because
it won the
race,
even though
it did have
to cheat.

profound saying 2

When love
and death kiss,
the result
is a human being.

family portrait 2

Three skinny
crumbs
of bread
whose eyes
are crystallized
tears.

family portrait 1

A father tombstone,
a mother tombstone,
a baby tombstone.

poem 1: the man who turned into a top

Jake whirled
around and around
in a sad, lonely
circle for
thirty-six years.

One day
he whirled so fast
that he turned
into a top,
whereupon the
circle immediately
changed into a
happy, beautiful
thing, and Jake
had so much fun
whirling
because
it
was not
a
man
anymore.

photograph 8

Eternity
picking its
teeth
with the cross
that Jesus
was crucified on.

photograph 3

A scared
idiot child
telling
his shadow
to
go away.

photograph 10

A disenchanted
voodoo
incantation
sitting in a
chair of boredom
and reading
The Saturday
Evening Post.

still life 2

An empty
checkbook,
a new
dress,
and a bottle
of
aspirin.

profound saying 3

If your
girl's kisses
make you
feel
weak in
the knees,
she may be
a vampire.

photograph 4

Two railroad
tickets to nowhere.
And
nowhere.

photograph 6

A butterfly
taking
a shit.

poem 4: love poem

Sleeping
with her
is like
sleeping
with a
witch's
broom.

Her eyes
have all the
emotion
of sandpaper.

When I kiss
her, it is like
kissing a mouse
trap which
has
been sprung.

(I still cannot
figure out
why I love her
more than
anything.)

still life 3

A bible
and a grain
of salt.

story 1: in god's arms

I got up, crawled aways, and struck a match.
"What are you doing?" she asked.
"I want to see whose grave I'm making love on," I said.
The match went out.
"God-damn it!" I said.
"You're drunk," she said.
"I could be," I said, and struck another match.

"You're drunk," she said.

I read the writing on the tombstone: "James Carrol Brown, born August 9, 1875, died May 4, 1883. He's in God's arms now."

"You're drunk, honey," she said.

photograph 5

The mechanical
function which
is love
sitting
all by itself
and lonely
on
a pile
of ashes
that were once
people.

question 1

Is it
against
the law
to eat
ice cream
in hell?

photograph 4

Ernest Hemingway
and
three marlin

sitting at a table
and drinking
a bottle
of gin.

crawdads eating a sea lamprey

The delicate reflections of fir trees lay on the surface of the
clear pool.

•

There were eight crawdads eating a dead sea lamprey at the
bottom of the pool.

•

The crawdads were a deep red.
The sea lamprey was a bright blue.
A current in the pool caused the sea lamprey to move slowly
back and forth.
It looked as if the crawdads were eating the sea lamprey
alive.

•

"Madge!" I yelled. "Come here!"
"What?"
"Come here!"
She got up from the big rock where she had been sitting and
watching me fish.
"Come here!"
"I'm coming!" She ran along the edge of the creek towards
me.

•

"Look," I said, pointing at the bottom of the pool.
"What is it," Madge said, "a snake?"
"It's a sea lamprey."
"It looks like a huge snake. Ohhhh!" she said. "They're eat-
ing it alive."
"No, it's dead."

•

"Oh, it's horrible," Madge said. "Absolutely horrible."

"Yeah."

"It's horrible," she said. "I can't stand to look at it."

"Neither can I."

"I can't stand to look at it," she said.

•

We didn't say anything else for awhile.

We just stood there staring at the crawdads eating the sea lamprey.

a haunted child

The child was crying in her sleep. She cried in her sleep every night.

•

Her mother stared down at her.

Sometimes her mother woke her up, and sometimes she let her sleep.

•

When she woke up the child, the child would always stop crying, and she would have no idea that she had been crying.

•

The child would get mad at her mother for waking her up for no reason at all.

•

The child lay very still in bed, and continued to cry.

•

Her mother stared down at her and did not know what to do.

•

After a long time, she turned out the lamp and went away, leaving behind the sobs of a haunted child.

Poem for Little Mamma

Birdy-oes
haunt,
like pieces
of
real gone
confetti,
this here
crAAAzy
sunset,
whereas I
don't,
but wish I
could.

(Do you dig me,
little mamma?)

That Thing Which Walks the Earth

Suddenly
her blue
eyes
changed
into
black vases
and in
each
one of
them
there was
a bouquet
of
dead
swans.

A Deer-Hunting Memoir

The two bucks
were hanging
from a tree.
They were
covered from
the shoulders
down by canvas
to protect them
from the rain.
Their tongues
were sticking
out and their
eyes glowed.
The air
was sweet with
the smell of
juniper brush.
Slow drops
of rain
fell through
the beam
of the flashlight.

Poem for Whom I Love a Green-Colored True

I would like
to be
a little tiger
sound asleep
and purring
in the enchanted jungle
of your brown hair.

Called War

I never want
to go away
to a place
called War.

I don't think
you want
to go there either.

Untitled

There is a dark house.
"How dark is it?"
Who are you?
"I'm reading this book."
Oh.
"Do you mind?"
Are you going to buy a copy?
"I might."
O.K.
"Now will you tell me how dark the house is?"
Yeah. The house is very dark.
"What does that mean?"
It means that little children should not wear beards.
"What — what did you say?"
I said, "Why don't you go into the house and look around?"
"I thought you said 'Little children should not wear beards.'"
You must be hearing things.

mr. otto's sunday school class

Mr. Otto was a large man: six six, two hundred thirty pounds. He had black hair and a long nose. His eyes had a large capacity for gentleness or fierceness. His voice was either very loud or unbelievably soft.

•

Mr. Otto was an undertaker.

•

He was married to a crippled woman whom he adored and covered with kindness. During their married life, he never once raised his voice to her, and he made her happy as a crippled woman could be.

•

"Nick, would you like to be nailed to a cross?"

•

"No, sir," Nick said.

"You bet you wouldn't!" Mr. Otto said, and the room was quiet.

Every eye was on Mr. Otto.

•

"Bill, have you ever stepped on a nail?"

"Sure," Bill said.

"You know how that feels."

"Yeah."

"Jesus didn't say 'Oh, goody!' when they nailed Him on the cross."

•

Mr. Otto was killed June 3, 1938.

•

He was riding along in his hearse, singing "Leaning on the Everlasting Arms," when he was hit by a train.

one man's family

Lester Rubenstein listens to "One Man's Family."

•

Lester Rubenstein is twenty-six years old and has been listening to "One Man's Family" for a long time.

•

Lester Rubenstein lives by himself in a comfortable little apartment where he earns a living by tying flies for fishing and selling them to sporting goods stores.

•

Lester Rubenstein has never been fishing.

•

Lester Rubenstein is very shy and hates to be around people because he's afraid when he's around them.

•

Of course, Lester Rubenstein has never been out with a girl in his whole life.

•

Once Lester Rubenstein missed hearing "One Man's Family" and he cried for an hour.

a glass of beer

Toby was happy as he drove his car into the garage. He was very happy as he got out of the car and went into the kitchen. He didn't know why he was happy. He was just happy.

•

"Mabel! I'm home from work, honey! Mabel! Sweetie pie!"
There was no answer.
"Mabel! Sweetie pie!"
There was no answer.

•

Toby went into the front room.

Mabel was sitting in a chair. There was a stagnant dreamy expression on her face.

She was holding a glass of beer in her hand.

•

"YOU PROMISED!" Toby said.

•

"Hi honey," Mabel said softly.

•

Toby walked over to her, took the glass of beer out of her hand and tossed it through a window.

The window dissolved into falling glass.

•

Mabel looked at her empty hand.

She stared at her empty hand.

"Where did my beer go?" Mabel asked softly.

The Flower Picker

Love is an enchanted puzzle that you cannot put together, even if you are trying hard.

1. I wonder how Ed makes love to her.

2. Libby is very gentle.
   Do you remember a wind in your childhood,
   stirring softly your mother's hair?

   Well, Libby's soul makes that wind seem
   like a hurricane.

3. I wonder why I had to goof with her.
   Why did I have to teach her not to love me.

4. The first time I saw Libby, she had some brown
   goop on her face, and she was wearing a gray
   sweatshirt, which was big enough for both
   of us. At the same time. A lovely idea.

5. JESUS CHRIST! My soul screams when I
   think about somebody else making love to her.
   Some little boy. I believe his name is Ed.

6. I never got to stroke her.
   Or kiss her.
   Or hold her hand.
   Even.

   I did get to say over the telephone, "I like you," and
   she said, "You've said too much."

7. I wonder if I will get a second chance with her.

8. I want to go to the forest with Libby. In spring.
   And pick wildflowers.

9. What I want to know is: why is she 15 and I 21?

10. I want her body. I want to explore her
    body with kisses. I want to make her body
    purr like a cat. I want to walk into a
    dark house, her body, and turn on all the lights.

in death's heart

A door
in Death's heart
will open wide
and I will go
inside
and find
seven rooms
each as big
as God.

child of the lovers

I
was
a
drunk rainbow.

She
was
a
frightened moon. ·

We
had
one child.

He grew up
to be
a frosty
spring night.

she came along

I built
a house
of tears
behind
the eight ball,
and I lived
there for
ten thousand
centuries,
until she came
along
and burned

118

the house down
with
a match
called love.

image

These
white flowers
sprinkled
on the grass
are really
frightened
drops
of blood.

a twentieth-century dream

I got into bed
and closed my eyes
and the warm, black
nothingness of sleep
came
and picked up my soul
and held it tightly
for a time
that could have been
forever
or a few moments.

Then I dreamt
I lived in a valley
that was green and peaceful.

I lived on a farm
and had a wife
and three children.

One day three bombers came.

They came low
over the mountains.

When the bombers
were through
the valley
was
gone.

my ivory tower

My ivory tower
overlooks
a slaughterhouse
where hogs
scream and scream
because
they do not like
to have their
throats cut.

My ivory tower
overlooks
a little girl
who has
a toothbrush
that she calls
Marty,
and loves.

advertisement

For sale,
cheap,
206
slightly sticky
love poems,
written
by
a seventeen-year-old
poet.

Phone Death.

argument

I dreamt
that I met
Ernest Hemingway.

We had a terrible argument
in the dream
because
Ernest Hemingway
thought that he was
a better writer
than I am.

a christmas tree in a graveyard

Late
at night
downtown
is like

a Christmas tree
in
a
graveyard.

hunger for a star

I love,
deep and pure
as the river,
a star
named Mary.

She is pressed against
that window
of eternity
called the sky.

My arms
are only
a few feet long.

Nature Lover, or Something

I am
not particular.

I like whatever
the sky happens
to be doing at the time.

Index of Titles